This Book Belongs To:

_____

_____

I Spy with my little eye
Something beginning with ...

I Spy with my little eye
Something beginning with ...

A

Apatosaurus

Apatosaurus

I Spy with my little eye
Something beginning with ...

I Spy with my little eye
something beginning with ...

Brontosaurus

Brontosaurus

I Spy with my little eye
Something beginning with ...

I spy with my little eye
Something beginning with ...

Corythosaurus

Corythosaurus

I Spy with my little eye
Something beginning with ...

D

I spy with my little eye
Something beginning with ...

Deinonychus

Deinonychus

I Spy with my little eye
Something beginning with ...

E

Euoplocephalus

I Spy with my little eye
Something beginning with ...

Fabrosaurus

Fabrosaurus

I Spy with my little eye
Something beginning with ...

Gallimimus

Gallimimus

I Spy with my little eye
Something beginning with ...

Hadrosaurus

Hadrosaurus

I Spy with my little eye
Something beginning with ...

I spy with my little eye,
Something beginning with ...

Iguanodon

Iguanodon

I Spy with my little eye
Something beginning with ...

Juravenator

Juravenator

I Spy with my little eye Something beginning with ...

K

Kronosaurus

Kronosaurus

I Spy with my little eye Something beginning with ...

Liaoxiornis

I Spy with my little eye
Something beginning with ...

M

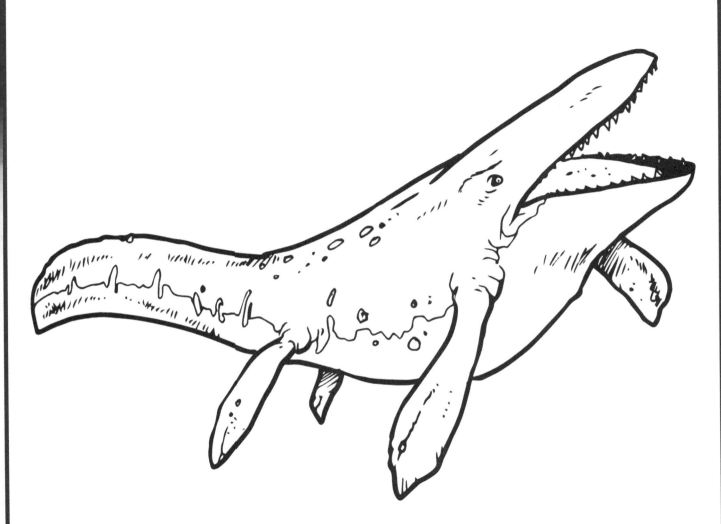

Mosasaurus

Mosasaurus

I Spy with my little eye Something beginning with ...

Nothronycus

Nothronycus

I Spy with my little eye Something beginning with ...

O

I Spy with my little eye

Something beginning with...

O

Ouranosaurus

Ouranosaurus

I Spy with my little eye Something beginning with ...

Pteranodon

Pteranodon

I Spy with my little eye
Something beginning with ...

Quaesitosaurus

I Spy with my little eye
Something beginning with ...

Rebbachisaurus

Rebbachisaurus

I Spy with my little eye Something beginning with ...

Stegosaurus

Stegosaurus

I Spy with my little eye Something beginning with ...

I spy with my little eye
Something beginning with ...

T

Triceratops

Triceratops

I Spy with my little eye
Something beginning with ...

Urbacodon

Urbacodon

I Spy with my little eye
Something beginning with ...

V

Velociraptor

Velociraptor

I Spy with my little eye
Something beginning with ...

Wuerhosaurus

Wuerthosaurus

I Spy with my little eye Something beginning with ...

I Spy with my little eye
Something beginning with...

X

Xenoceratops

I Spy with my little eye
Something beginning with ...

I Spy with my little eye
Something beginning with ...

Yinlong

I Spy with my little eye
Something beginning with ...

Zephyrosaurus

Zephyrosaurus

I hope you enjoyed
Leave us a feedback!
it's gone be helpfull to make
good books for your child

Made in the USA
Coppell, TX
01 November 2023

23671852R00059